Amazing Oreo Recipes

Hannie P. Scott
www.Hanniepscott.com

Copyright © 2016 Hannie P. Scott
All rights reserved.

No part of this book may be reproduced in any form without written permission from the author. Reviewers may quote brief excerpts from the book in reviews.

Disclaimer: No part of this publication may be reproduced or transmitted in any form, mechanical or electronic, including photocopied or recorded, or by any information storage and retrieval system, or transmitted by email without permission in writing or email from the author or publisher.

While attempts have been made to verify all information provided in this publication, neither the author nor the publisher assumes any responsibility for errors, omissions, or contrary interpretations of the subjects discussed.

This book is for entertainment purposes only. The views expressed are those of the author alone and should not be taken as expert instructions or commands. The reader is responsible for his/her own actions.

Adherence to all applicable laws and regulations, including international, federal, state, and local government, or any other jurisdiction is the sole responsibility of the purchaser or reader.

Neither the author nor the publisher assume any responsibility or liability whatsoever on the behalf of the purchaser or reader of these materials.

ISBN-13: 978-1537685083
ISBN-10: 1537685082

> *One of the very nicest things about life is the way we must regularly stop whatever we are doing and devote our attention to eating.*

LUCIANO PAVAROTTI

CONTENTS

- Abbreviations 3
- Conversions 3
- Peppermint Dipped Oreos 5
- Christmas Cookie Bark 6
- Oreo Balls 7
- Oreo Peppermint Bark 8
- Frozen Peppermint Pie 9
- Oreo Peppermint Cookies 10
- Chocolate Peppermint Cookies 11
- Oreo Dirt Cake 13
- Oreo Rice Krispie Treats 14
- Hoot Owl Pretzels 15
- Oreo Peanut Butter Popcorn 16
- Peanut Butter Pie 17
- Oreo Cheesecake Cookies 18
- Oreo Pops 19
- Cookies and Cream Cupcakes 20
- Oreo Dirt Cake Truffle 22
- Red Velvet Dirt Cake 23
- Oreo Poke Cake 25
- Cookies and Cream Blondies 26
- Oreo Pie 28
- No Bake Oreo Delight 29
- Oreo Fudge 30
- Fried Oreos 31
- Oreo Bark 32
- Oreo Truffles 33
- FREE GIFT 35
- NOTES 36

FREE GIFT

Breakfast, Lunch, Dinner, Soups, Salads, Desserts and More!

To download your free eBook, simply visit:
www.Hanniepscott.com/freegift

Abbreviations

oz = ounce
fl oz = fluid ounce
tsp = teaspoon
tbsp = tablespoon
ml = milliliter
c = cup
pt = pint
qt = quart
gal = gallon
L = liter

Conversions

1/2 fl oz = 3 tsp = 1 tbsp = 15 ml
1 fl oz = 2 tbsp = 1/8 c = 30 ml
2 fl oz = 4 tbsp = 1/4 c = 60 ml
4 fl oz = 8 tbsp = 1/2 c = 118 ml
8 fl oz = 16 tbsp = 1 c = 236 ml
16 fl oz = 1 pt = 1/2 qt = 2 c = 473 ml
128 fl oz = 8 pt = 4 qt = 1 gal = 3.78 L

Peppermint Dipped Oreos

Servings: 10-12

What you need:
1 package Oreos
1 package vanilla candy melts
1 package peppermint baking chips
Crushed soft peppermints

What to do:
1. In a microwave safe bowl, combine the vanilla candy melts and the peppermint baking chips for 3 minutes, stirring every 30 seconds.
2. Dip each Oreo into the melted mixture then sprinkle with crushed peppermints.
3. Let cool on a sheet of wax paper before serving.

Christmas Cookie Bark

Servings: 16-18

What you need:
14 Christmas Oreos, broken into pieces
1 1/2 cups pretzels, broken into pieces
1 cup Christmas colored M&M's
1 lb white chocolate or almond bark
Christmas colored sprinkles

What to do:
1. Line a baking sheet with parchment paper.
2. Mix together the Oreo pieces, pretzels, and 3/4 cup of the M&M's.
3. Melt the white chocolate or bark in a microwave safe bowl for 2-3 minutes, stirring every 30 seconds until completely melted.
4. Drizzle the melted chocolate over the mixture on the baking sheet.
5. Top the chocolate with the rest of the M&M's and sprinkles.
6. Allow the bark to cool before breaking up and serving.

Oreo Balls

Servings: 24

What you need:
15.5-oz package of Oreos
8 oz of cream cheese, softened
3/4 lb vanilla almond bark, chopped
Christmas colored sprinkles

What to do:
1. Line a baking sheet with parchment paper.
2. Place the Oreos in a food processor and pulse until finely chopped.
3. Place the chopped Oreos in a large bowl and add in the cream cheese. Mix well.
4. Roll the mixture into 24 balls and place on the prepared baking sheet.
5. Place the baking sheet into your refrigerator for at least 30 minutes or until the balls are firm.
6. In a microwave safe bowl, melt the almond bark in the microwave for 2 minutes, stirring every 30 seconds.
7. Place a skewer or toothpick into the Oreo balls and dip into the melted almond bark until coated.
8. Cover the balls with sprinkles and place back onto the baking sheet.
9. Let the balls cool for at least 30 minutes before serving.

Oreo Peppermint Bark

Servings: 15

What you need:
10 mini candy canes, crushed
12 Oreos, chopped
1 cup chocolate chips
1 1/2 cups white chocolate chips

What to do:
1. Line a baking sheet with parchment paper and spray with non-stick spray.
2. Add the milk chocolate chips to a microwave safe bowl and microwave for 30 second intervals until smooth and melted. Stir between every 30 second interval.
3. Pour the melted chocolate onto the prepared pan and spread it evenly.
4. Sprinkle the chopped Oreos on the warm chocolate and chill for 10 minutes.
5. Add the white chocolate to a microwave safe bowl and microwave for 30 second intervals until smooth and melted. Stir between every interval.
6. Pour the melted white chocolate over the Oreos and spread evenly.
7. Sprinkle the chopped candy canes over the warm white chocolate.
8. Chill until completely set then break into pieces.

Frozen Peppermint Pie

Servings: 16

What you need:
2 premade Oreo cookie pie crusts
8 oz whipped cream, thawed
1.5 quart container of peppermint ice cream
Crushed candy canes
8 Oreos, crushed

What to do:
1. Soften the ice cream until it can be easily mixed.
2. Mix the ice cream and whipped cream.
3. Spread the mixture into the two pie crusts.
4. Freeze for several hours then top with crushed candy canes and crushed Oreos.

Oreo Peppermint Cookies

Makes 36 cookies

What you need:
1 box white cake mix
1 stick butter, melted
1 egg
1/2 tsp peppermint extract
1/2 tsp vanilla extract
4 oz cream cheese, softened and cubed
1 cup crushed Oreos
1 cup Andes Peppermint Crunch pieces
1/2 cup chocolate chips

What to do:
1. In a mixing bowl, combine the cake mix, melted butter, egg, peppermint extract, and vanilla extract. Beat until a dough forms.
2. Add the cream cheese to the dough and mix until combined.
3. Stir in the peppermint crunch pieces and chocolate chips.
4. Stir in the crushed Oreos gently.
5. Refrigerate the dough for 30 minutes.
6. Preheat your oven to 350 degrees F and line a baking sheet or two with parchment paper and spray with non-stick spray.
7. Roll the dough into balls and line them 1-inch apart on the prepared pans.
8. Bake for 9-10 minutes.
9. Remove the pans from the oven and let the cookies sit for 2 minutes before transferring to a wire rack or a sheet of wax paper to cool completely.

Chocolate Peppermint Cookies

Servings: 15

What you need:
3/4 cup butter, softened
1/2 cup brown sugar, packed
1/2 cup sugar
1 egg
1/2 tsp vanilla extract
1/2 tsp peppermint extract
1 1/4 cups all-purpose flour
1/2 cup cocoa
1 tsp baking soda
1/2 cup Andes Peppermint Crunch pieces
3/4 cup chopped Oreos

What to do:
1. In a mixing bowl, cream together the butter and sugar until light and fluffy.
2. Mix in the egg and vanilla extract.
3. In a separate bowl, whisk together the flour, cocoa, and baking powder until combined.
4. Gradually add the flour mixture to the butter and sugar mixture and mix until combined well.
5. Cover and refrigerate for at least an hour.
6. Preheat your oven to 350 degrees F and line a baking sheet with parchment paper.
7. Form the dough into 1-2 inch balls and place them on the baking sheet 1-inch apart.

8. Bake for 8-10 minutes or until the edges look firm. The middle should still look soft.
9. Remove from the oven and cool for 2 minutes before transferring to a wire rack to cool completely.

Oreo Dirt Cake

Serves: 8-10

What you need:
1 package Oreos, crushed
8 oz cream cheese, softened
1/4 cup butter
1 cup powdered sugar
3 cups milk
2 small packages instant vanilla pudding mix
1/2 tsp vanilla extract
12 oz cool whip, thawed

What to do:
1. Cream together cream cheese, butter, and powdered sugar in a large bowl.
2. In a separate bowl, mix together milk, pudding, vanilla extract, and cool whip.
3. Add cream cheese mixture to pudding mixture.
4. Layer with Oreos in a large glass serving bowl.

Oreo Rice Krispie Treats

Serves: 10-12

What you need:
3 tbsp butter
4 cups mini marshmallows
6 cups rice krispies cereal
15 Halloween Oreos, crushed

What to do:
1. Melt the butter over low heat in a large saucepan.
2. Add marshmallows and stir completely until they are all melted then remove the heat.
3. Pour rice krispies and Oreos into a large bowl and mix together.
4. Spray some cooking spray onto a spatula and add marshmallows to the bowl with rice krispies and Oreos and stir until combined.
5. Gently press mixture into a 13 x 9 inch pan that is coated with cooking spray.
6. Let them cool then cut into squares.

Hoot Owl Pretzels

Serves: 10-12

What you need:
1 bag large pretzels
White chocolate almond bark or candy melts
Mini Oreos
Black sprinkles
Black icing gel
Black licorice
Chocolate chips

What to do:
1. Melt almond bark/candy melts according to package directions.
2. Dip large pretzel into the melted almond bark and place on baking sheet lined with parchment paper.
3. Lightly sprinkle the sprinkles onto the covered pretzel.
4. Separate the mini Oreos and place one half on each top rounded part on each pretzel.
5. Drop a small round blob of the melted almond bark/candy melt onto the center of each Oreo and place a chocolate chip on each blob.
6. Draw a beak with the black icing gel between the two Oreo eyes (slightly lower).
7. Draw feet onto the bottom of the pretzel with the black icing gel.
8. Cut the black licorice into small pieces and use as eyebrows.

Oreo Peanut Butter Popcorn

Serves: 4-6

What you need:
1 bag microwave popcorn
8 oz vanilla almond bark
1/4 cup peanut butter
16 Oreos, coarsely chopped

What to do:
1. Pop the popcorn according to the package directions.
2. Pour popped popcorn into a large bowl and remove any unpopped kernels.
3. Place vanilla almond bark in microwave safe bowl and heat for one minute.
4. Stir vanilla and add peanut butter.
5. Microwave for about a minute more, stopping at 30 seconds to stir.
6. Once vanilla and peanut butter are completely melted together, slowly pour the mixture over the popcorn and stir carefully.
7. Add chopped Oreos and toss.
8. Pour popcorn out onto a baking sheet lined with parchment paper and let cool until hardened.
9. Serve or store in airtight container.

Peanut Butter Pie

Serves: 6-8

What you need:
1 package Oreos
4 tbsp butter, melted
1 cup peanut butter
8 oz cream cheese, softened
1 cup powdered sugar
8 oz cool whip, thawed

What to do:
1. Preheat your oven to 350 degrees F.
2. Place Oreos into a food processor and pulse until they're fine crumbs.
3. Add the melted butter to the Oreo crumbs and stir with a fork to combine.
4. Press into a pie pan and bake for 7 minutes or until set. Then allow to cool completely.
5. In a large mixing bowl, combine peanut butter and cream cheese and beat until smoothed together.
6. Add the powdered sugar and beat until combined.
7. Add the cool whip and mix until combined.
8. Pour into the crust and smooth the top.
9. Chill for at least 2 hours before serving.

Oreo Cheesecake Cookies

Servings: 12

What you need:
4 oz cream cheese, softened
8 tbsp salted butter, softened
3/4 cup sugar
1 cup all-purpose flour
10 Oreos, broken into pieces

What to do:
1. Beat the cream cheese and butter until fluffy with a mixer in a large bowl.
2. Add in the sugar and mix well.
3. Add in the flour, a little bit at a time on low until combined.
4. Fold in the Oreos with a spoon.
5. Cover the bowl and refrigerate for 30 minutes or freeze for 10 minutes.
6. Preheat your oven to 350 degrees F and line a large baking sheet with parchment paper.
7. Drop 2 tbsp sized balls of dough onto the baking sheet.
8. Bake for 9-11 minutes or until barely golden at the edges.
9. Remove from the oven and cool for 5 minutes, then transfer them to a cooling rack to cool completely before serving

Oreo Pops

Servings: 24

What you need:
White melting chocolate
1 package of Oreo's
Valentine's sprinkles
Sucker sticks

What to do:
1. Melt the chocolate according to package directions.
2. Carefully remove one side of each Oreo and place a sucker stick in the filling. You can also place a small amount of melted chocolate on the stick to make it stay together better.
3. Put the side of the Oreo you took off back.
4. Dip the Oreo into the melted chocolate.
5. Quickly sprinkle the sprinkles on the chocolate dipped Oreo.
6. Place on a sheet of wax paper to dry completely.

Cookies and Cream Cupcakes

Servings: 24

What you need:
--Cupcake batter:
2 cups flour
2 tbsp cake flour
1/2 tsp salt
2 tsp baking powder
1/2 cup butter, softened
1 cup sugar
2 eggs
1 cup milk
1 tbsp vanilla extract

--Frosting:
1 package Oreos
1 cup unsalted butter
1 tbsp vanilla extract
¼ cup heavy cream
6 cups powdered sugar

What to do:
1. Preheat your oven to 375 degrees F.
2. Line a cupcake pan with liners.
3. With an electric mixer, blend the butter and sugar until fluffy.
4. Beat in the eggs slowly.
5. In a separate bowl, mix together the flour, baking powder, and salt.

6. Slowly add the dry ingredients to the wet ingredients.
7. Slowly mix in the vanilla and milk.
8. Scoop ½ cup of the batter into each liner.
9. Bake for 20 minutes.
10. While the cupcakes are baking, mix together the powdered sugar and butter for the frosting until crumbly.
11. Mix in the vanilla.
12. Mix in the heavy cream 2 tbsp at a time until the frosting starts to get creamy.
13. Put the Oreos in a ziplock bag (or food processor) and crush them.
14. Stir the crushed Oreos into the frosting.
15. When the cupcakes are finished baking, remove them from the oven and let them cool completely.
16. After they are cooled, frost them and serve!

Oreo Dirt Cake Truffle

Servings: 12

What you need:
1/2 cup butter
8 oz whipped cream
1 package Oreos
2 packages instant pudding
8 oz cream cheese, softened
1 cup powdered sugar
3 1/2 cups milk

What to do:
1. With an electric mixer, cream together butter, cream cheese, and powdered sugar in a large bowl.
2. In a separate bowl, whisk the pudding, milk, and Cool Whip.
3. Add the pudding mixture into the cream cheese mixture and mix well.
4. Crush the Oreos either in your food processor or in a large zip lock bag.
5. Layer the cookie and pudding mixture in a trifle bowl and chill in the refrigerator for 1 hour before serving.

Red Velvet Dirt Cake

Servings: 12

What you need:
2 1/2 cups all-purpose flour
1 tsp baking powder
1 tsp salt
2 tbsp unsweetened cocoa powder
2 oz. red food coloring
1/2 cup unsalted butter, at room temperature
1 1/2 cups sugar
2 eggs, at room temperature
1 tsp vanilla extract
1 cup buttermilk, at room temperature
1 tsp white vinegar
1 tsp baking soda
2 8-oz blocks of cream cheese
1/3 cup sugar
2 cups heavy whipping cream

What to do:
1. Preheat your oven to 350 degrees F.
2. Butter and flour two 9-inch round cake pans.
3. Sift together the flour, baking powder and salt and set aside.
4. In a small bowl, mix together the food coloring and cocoa powder to form a paste.
5. In a large bowl, beat the butter and sugar together until light and fluffy with a hand mixer.
6. One at a time, beat in the eggs.

7. Mix in the vanilla and the red cocoa paste.
8. Add the flour mixture slowly and mix well.
9. Add the buttermilk slowly and mix well.
10. In a small bowl, mix together the vinegar and baking soda then add the mixture to the cake batter and stir well.
11. Divide the cake batter evenly between the 2 cake pans and bake for 25-30 minutes or until a toothpick inserted comes out clean.
12. Remove the cakes from the oven and allow them to cool completely in the pans.
13. While the cakes are cooling, beat the cream cheese and sugar in a large bowl with an electric mixer until fluffy and light.
14. On low speed, slowly pour in the whipping cream and mix until the mixture is soft and creamy. It might take up to 10 minutes. This makes the frosting!
15. Arrange a single layer of red velvet cake chunks to the bottom of a trifle dish and top it with 1/3 of the frosting.
16. Repeat the layers two more times and top with red velvet cake.
17. Refrigerate for 1 hour before serving.

Oreo Poke Cake

Servings: 10

What you need:
1 box chocolate cake mix, plus ingredients called for
2 4-oz packages of instant Oreo pudding
2 cups milk
10-15 crushed Oreos

What to do:
1. Mix the cake according to directions on the box.
2. Bake in a well-greased 9x13 pan and bake according to package directions.
3. When the cake has about 5 minutes before it is finished baking, mix together the pudding. In a medium bowl, pour both pudding mixtures and mix with 2 cups milk. Whisk until most of the lumps are gone.
4. When the cake is finished baking, remove it from the oven and poke holes all over it. I used the end of a wooden spoon.
5. Pour the pudding mixture over the warm cake, filling the holes with the mixture.
6. Cover and let the cake refrigerate for at least an hour.
7. Sprinkle crushed Oreos on top of the cake before serving.

Cookies and Cream Blondies

Servings: 10

What you need:
1 cup butter, softened
1 cup brown sugar
1/2 cup sugar
2 eggs
1 tsp vanilla
1 package vanilla instant pudding
2 cups flour
1 tsp baking soda
1/2 tsp baking powder
1 tsp salt
1 cup chocolate chips
1 cup white chocolate chips
16 Oreos, broken into pieces

What to do:
1. Preheat your oven to 350 degrees F and grease a 9x13 pan.
2. In a large bowl with an electric mixer, cream together the butter, brown sugar, and sugar.
3. Add the eggs and vanilla and mix well.
4. Add the dry pudding mix and mix well.
5. Add the flour, baking soda, baking powder, and salt until well mixed.
6. Fold in the chocolate chips, white chocolate chips, and Oreo pieces.

7. Pour the batter into the prepared pan and bake for 20-22 minutes or until a toothpick inserted comes out clean.
8. Allow to cool, cut, then serve.

Oreo Pie

Servings: 8

What you need:

1 package Oreos
1/2 stick butter, melted
1 1/2 cups milk
2 packages vanilla instant pudding
8 oz whipped cream, thawed

What to do:

1. Crush 25 Oreos in your blender or food processor.
2. Mix the crushed Oreos with the melted butter and press the mixture into a 9-inch pie plate.
3. In a large bowl, whisk together the milk and vanilla pudding.
4. Stir the whipped cream into the pudding.
5. Roughly chop all but 6 of the Oreos and stir into the pudding.
6. Spoon the pudding mixture into the pie crust.
7. Garnish with the rest of the Oreos.
8. Refrigerate for at least 4 hours.

No Bake Oreo Delight

Servings: 10

What you need:
1 package of Oreos
1 cup of milk
16 oz whipped cream, thawed
8 oz cream cheese, softened

What to do:
1. Have a 9x13 baking dish nearby.
2. Place the cream cheese in a large bowl and mix it with an electric mixer until it is light and fluffy.
3. Add the whipped cream to the cream cheese and mix well. Set aside.
4. Dip 15-18 Oreos, one at a time, in the milk and place them in an even layer in the bottom of the baking dish.
5. Pour half of the cream cheese mixture on top of the Oreos and spread evenly.
6. Dip the other half of the Oreos in the milk, one at a time, and layer them evenly on top of the cream cheese mixture.
7. Pour the other half of the cream cheese over the Oreos and spread evenly.
8. Cover and refrigerate for 2 hours before serving.

Oreo Fudge

Servings: 12

What you need:
1 8-oz package of cream cheese, at room temp
4 cups powdered sugar
1 1/2 tsp vanilla extract
15 oz white chocolate, roughly chopped
15 Oreos, roughly chopped

What to do:
1. In a large bowl with an electric mixer, beat the cream cheese, powdered sugar, and vanilla until smooth and fluffy.
2. Place the white chocolate in a microwave safe bowl and heat in the microwave for 30 seconds at a time until smooth and melted.
3. Stir the melted white chocolate and 3/4 of the chopped Oreos into the cream cheese mixture.
4. Line a baking dish with parchment paper.
5. Spread the mixture into the baking dish.
6. Press the remaining Oreos into the fudge.
7. Cover and refrigerate for 3-4 hours.
8. Cut into small squares and serve or store in an airtight container in the fridge.

Fried Oreos

Servings: 10

What you need:
10 Oreos
1 cup pancake mix
1/2 cup milk
1 egg
Powdered sugar
Vegetable Oil

What to do:
1. In a small bowl, mix together the pancake mix, milk, and egg until combined and few lumps remain.
2. Add 1 inch of vegetable oil into a deep, heavy pan and heat over medium-high heat.
3. When the oil is hot, dip an Oreo into the pancake batter and make sure the Oreo is well coated.
4. Place the Oreo into the hot oil and cook for 30 seconds to 1 minute on each side until the batter is golden brown.
5. Repeat with all of the Oreos.
6. Sprinkle powdered sugar over the fried Oreos and serve immediately.

Oreo Bark

Servings: 12

What you need:
10 oz white chocolate chips
18 Oreos

What to do:
1. Melt the chocolate chips in a microwave safe bowl in the microwave at 30 second intervals until melted and smooth.
2. Chop 15 of the Oreos and stir them into the melted white chocolate.
3. Line a baking pan with parchment paper and spread the chocolate/Oreo mixture onto the pan.
4. Finely chop the remaining 3 Oreos and sprinkle them over the Oreo bark.

Oreo Truffles

Makes 36 balls

What you need:
8 oz package cream cheese, at room temperature
1 package Oreos
12 oz white chocolate chips

What to do:
1. Crush the Oreos in your blender or food processor. Reserve 2 tbsp of the crushed Oreos for garnish.
2. Cut the cream cheese into cubes and place it in the blender or food processor with the crushed Oreos and blend well.
3. Shape the mixture into 36 balls.
4. Place the balls on a baking sheet and place in your freezer for 10-30 minutes or your refrigerator for 1-2 hours.
5. Melt the chocolate chips in a microwave safe bowl in the microwave at 30 second intervals until melted and smooth.
6. Using two forks, dip each chocolate ball into the melted chocolate. Fully coat each ball then place it on a sheet of wax paper to dry.
7. Let truffles cool completely before serving.

FREE GIFT

Breakfast, Lunch, Dinner, Soups, Salads, Desserts and More!

To download your free eBook, simply visit:
www.Hanniepscott.com/freegift

NOTES

NOTES

NOTES

NOTES

Printed in Poland
by Amazon Fulfillment
Poland Sp. z o.o., Wrocław